Substitute Teacher

Put everything you need in one folder for a successful day of substitute teaching!

For the Classroom Teacher:

- In the case of your absence, notify your supervisor as soon as possible.
- Cancel or reschedule any parent meetings or after-school activities.
- If possible, leave your keys in the main office.
- Keep the contents of this folder up-to-date.

For the Substitute Teacher:

- Substitute Teacher Daily Report: Make copies of this form and fill one out each day to notify the classroom teacher about the happenings in the classroom.
- Quick Awards: Copy these awards onto colored paper, cut apart, and hand them out to deserving students.
- Learning Activities and Reproducible Pages: These fun activities and reproducible pages can be copied and easily adapted to a variety of grade levels. They need little preparation and help fill in those moments when students finish their work early or just for fun!

How to Be a Great
Substitute Teacher!

Here are a few ideas to help you have a happy, productive day.

Before School Begins:
- Arrive at school thirty minutes early.
- Acquaint yourself with the day's lesson plans and prepare for any special happenings or specific instructions.
- Prepare copies of any materials left by the teacher.
- Write your name on the class board, as well as any instructions from the teacher.
- Familiarize yourself with the teacher's schedule, including recess, lunch, and dismissal times. (You may want to post this on the class board.)
- Greet the students at the door with a smile.
- Familiarize yourself with any safety procedures, student allergies, or any student's special needs.

First Few Minutes:
- Introduce yourself to the students.
- Take attendance and lunch count.
- Tell them a little about yourself, such as your hobbies, interests, family, etc.
- Read to the class any pertinent information or instructions from the teacher.
- Remind the students that they know the class expectations to follow all class rules and procedures. Express confidence that they will do so.

Throughout the Day:
- Keep the students working. Follow the lesson plans, but also have available activities for students that finish early.
- Tell students when they are well-behaved or are working well.
- Make sure each student receives some positive feedback from you. It is important that the students know that you like them and enjoy being part of their class for the day.

Discipline:
- If you need to discipline a student, follow the procedures left by the teacher.
- Take control of the class by being firm and confident. Give a warning before disciplining a student; however, don't give too many "second chances." The first warning should be sufficient.
- Never lose your temper! Keep your cool and use a quiet and firm voice.
- Maintain eye contact when speaking to students.
- Try to remember and use the students' names. They will be more cooperative if they think you know them personally.
- When dismissing students either for recess or at the end of the day, do it in an orderly manner. A suggestion might be to say, "Those wearing the color green may line up," or "Those who have a 'g' in their name may be dismissed."
- Contact another teacher or an administrator if a problem persists.

End of the Day:
- Fill out a "Substitute Teacher Daily Report" form and go over it with the students to prevent misunderstandings.
- Pass out special "Substitute Teacher Helper Awards" to deserving students.
- Make sure students clearly understand what homework has been assigned.
- Check in with the school's office before leaving for the day.
- Now, go home and relax. You deserve it!

Substitute Teacher Daily Report

School _________________________   Classroom Teacher _________________________

Date _______________ Grade _________   Substitute Teacher _________________________

These Students Were Absent:

_____________   _____________

_____________   _____________

_____________   _____________

_____________   _____________

The Following Students:

Were Helpful   Disruptive

_________________   _________________

_________________   _________________

_________________   _________________

The Class…

☐ was helpful and courteous.   ☐ followed classroom rules.

☐ worked well on assignments.   ☐ _________________________

Assignments Not Completed:

1. ____

2. ____

3. ____

Additional Comments: ____________________________________

____

____

____

Next Time, I Would Appreciate the Following: ________________

____

Signed _________________________

Classroom Schedule

Teacher _________________________ Room _____________ Date_______________

<table>
<tr><td>

Morning

7:00 _______________

____

7:30 _______________

____

8:00 _______________

____

8:30 _______________

____

9:00 _______________

____

9:30 _______________

____

10:00 _______________

____

10:30 _______________

____

11:00 _______________

____

11:30 _______________

____

</td><td>

Afternoon

12:00 _______________

____

12:30 _______________

____

1:00 _______________

____

1:30 _______________

____

2:00 _______________

____

2:30 _______________

____

3:00 _______________

____

3:30 _______________

____

4:00 _______________

____

4:30 _______________

____

</td></tr>
</table>

Duty Schedule ____

____

This Week's Lesson Plans

Week of ____

Teacher _________________________________ Room _______________

M O N D A Y	
T U E S D A Y	
W E D N E S D A Y	
T H U R S D A Y	
F R I D A Y	

Things You Need to Know

Classroom Procedures

Attendance ______________________

____

____

____

Lunch Count/Money ______________________

____

____

____

Lunch/Recess ______________________

____

____

____

Restroom/Hall Pass/Nurse

____

____

____

Emergency Drills ______________________

____

____

____

Media Center ______________________

____

____

____

Rainy Day ______________________

____

____

____

Dismissal ______________________

____

____

____

Classroom Management (See copies of the school and classroom rules.)

Discipline ______________________

____

____

____

Consequences ______________________

____

____

____

Rewards ______________________

____

____

____

Serious Behavior ______________________

____

____

____

Things You Need to Know

Student Schedules
(Students attending special classes, in need of medication, special circumstances, etc.)

Name	Purpose	Location	Day	Time

If You Need Help . . .

Teacher   Room #

_______________________   _______________

_______________________   _______________

_______________________   _______________

_______________________   _______________

Reliable Students . . .

____

____

Notes

____

____

____

____

____

____

____

____

Things You Need to Know

Student Allergies

Student Name	Type of Allergy	Notes

People to Know (other teachers, administrators, staff)

Name	Title	Contact Information

Technology Use Procedures

____

____

____

Approved Websites and Apps

Title	Notes

____
Name

was a great help in class today!

___________________   ___________________
Teacher   Date

____
Date

____
Student

____
Teacher

Awarded To

____
Name

____
Name

Completed All Assignments Today!

___________________   ___________________
Teacher   Date

Seating Chart

Teacher ____ Room _______________ Date_______________

Draw in your own seating chart. You may want to use small stick-on notes to denote desks complete with students' names. The notes can easily be moved or changed throughout the year. Include other important elements such as centers, supply bins, etc.

Fun, Low-Prep Learning Activities

Three-Minute Word Game

Choose an interesting word (the longer the better) and write it in large letters on the class board. Pronounce the word for students and tell them its meaning. Instruct them to get out a piece of paper and pencil. Using a timer, give them three minutes to write as many words as possible using only the letters in the word on the board. When time is up, have students exchange papers and check the accuracy of each word. The winner is the student who has come up with the most correct words and can tell you the meaning of the original word. Here are some words you might use:

SPAGHETTI	THERMOMETER
EVAPORATE	AUTOMATIC
MASQUERADE	MARIONETTE
HORIZONTAL	VERTICAL
SILHOUETTE	JOURNALISM
ORCHESTRA	SUBSCRIPTION
PROSPERITY	RESPONSIBILITY
SCHOLARSHIP	SENTIMENTAL
RECTANGLE	TRANSPORT
INVENTION	ASTRONAUT

Read-for-All

Give students extra time to read high-interest picture books of their choice. Make this free reading time more special by allowing students to choose favorite spots in the classroom to read or to read with a friend or reading partner. Have students write and draw a short sequel for their favorite picture book to share with the class.

That's a Fact

Boost automaticity of math facts by giving students extra time to practice. Have students play Fact War in pairs. In this game, each student lays down a playing card. Whichever student is first to correctly call out the sum or product (depending on grade) of the two cards keeps both cards. The student who has the most cards wins.

Math Bingo

Have students fold a sheet of paper to create a 4 by 4 grid. Students then write one number in each box. For younger grades, have students choose numbers up to 25. Older students may choose numbers up to 50 or beyond. Once students have filled in their boxes with different numbers, you are ready to begin. Call out math problems with answers that range up to 25 (for younger students) or 50+ (for older students). If students have the answer in one of their boxes, they may mark the number with a pencil. For example, if you call out 14 + 25, students who have 39 on their grid will mark that number. The first student to get four numbers in a row on their grid wins.

Secret Code

Tell students that you are going to write a secret message on the class board and give them 5 minutes to decipher it. Write these numbers on the board:

20, 15, 13, 15, 18, 18, 15, 23 / 9, 19 /
20, 8, 5 / 6, 9, 18, 19, 20 / 4, 1, 25 /
15, 6 / 20, 8, 5 / 18, 5, 19, 20 / 15, 6 /
25, 15, 21, 18 / 12, 9, 6, 5!

Tell students that each letter in the message represents a letter of the alphabet, (1 = a, 2 = b, 3 = c, etc.) The winner is the student who can decipher the message first. Encourage students to then write their own messages for the class to figure out. (The message is: "Tomorrow is the first day of the rest of your life!")

Spelling Bingo

Write students' spelling or vocabulary words on the class board. Instruct students to fold a sheet of paper so that when it is open there are 12 squares. (Fold the paper in thirds and then in half twice.) Tell students to randomly write the words, one in each square. Children can use small scraps of paper as markers. Play Spelling Bingo by calling out the words until one student yells, "BINGO!"

Make-a-Word

On the class board, write the beginning and final letters of several four-letter words and see how many words students can come up with in a specific amount of time. Examples might be:

    L _ _ E   (love, like, late, lake, etc.)
    W _ _ D   (weed, word, wild, etc.)
    R _ _ E   (ripe, rope, rise, rose, etc.)

The winner is the one with the most correct words.

Dear Miss Gabby

Instruct students to write a letter to an imaginary "Miss Gabby" about a problem they have or have heard about. The situations can be serious or just for fun. Tell them not to include names and to not sign their name to the letter. Collect all the letters, then draw several from the stack to read. Discuss with students the possible ways the problems might be solved.

Substitute Student

Spark students' imagination and challenge their critical thinking skills with this simple activity.

Tell students that they are to imagine the following: Instead of coming to school and finding a substitute teacher in place of their regular teacher, their teacher has come to school and found substitute students!

Have students write want ads for substitute students who could take their places. Make sure they list duties, skills, and qualifications that would be necessary to do the job.

Quickie Activities

Here are a few "quickie" learning activities you can use to fill in those few minutes before the next activity or when students finish an activity faster than you expected.

Reading/Language Arts
- List 20 compound words.
- Write a new ending to the story of "The Three Pigs."
- List as many "color" words as possible. Put them in alphabetical order.
- Write a poem about popcorn.

Math/Problem Solving
- Draw a diagram to show how to divide 27 jelly beans equally among three friends.
- If a man died at age 63 in 2006, in what year was he born? If he were still alive today, how old would he be?
- How many "legs" are in this classroom? (Make sure students include table and chair legs, legs of any pets, etc.)

Science
- Name six animals that swim.
- Name five things that can be recycled or reused.
- List eight healthy snack foods.
- List as many words as possible to best describe the observations made with each of our five senses.

Social Studies
- Name a country in Europe, a country in South America, a country in Africa, etc.
- Name three past presidents.
- Name a person who invented something and tell what it was.
- Tell one way you are like everyone else and one way you are different.

The Teacher Is Missing!

The appearance of a substitute in the classroom is a perfect opportunity to introduce Harry Allard's delightful book, published by Houghton-Mifflin, ©1987, *Miss Nelson Is Missing!* (Substitutes may want to buy their own copy or they may find it in most libraries.)

The story revolves around the disappearance of the kindly teacher Miss Nelson and her replacement with the tough-as-nails substitute, Miss Viola Swamp. Through humorous twists and turns, the readers, but not the students in the story, discover that Miss Swamp is really Miss Nelson in disguise.

Before reading the story, prepare the class by asking them what feelings they have when they come to class and discover that the regular teacher is absent and they have a substitute teacher. Ask them to suggest reasons why a regular teacher may miss school. Then tell them that the story you are about to read is about a rather unusual substitute.

After reading the story aloud, ask the children the following questions:

- What qualities do you like most about your teacher?
- Why do you think Miss Nelson disguised herself as a substitute teacher?
- How are you like the students in the story? How are you different?

What a Character!

Students will love making their own mini-books about a favorite character from their reading. This could be from a class read-aloud or from students' independent reading books. Make a class set of the reproducible mini-book on pages 15 and 16. For older students, emphasize the importance of using text evidence to support their ideas as they complete the mini-book. Have extra paper available for students to add on pages as needed.

For children who are not yet writing, help them use a read-aloud to describe their character. Rather then use the reproducible template, have students use drawing paper and make a four- or six-page booklet. Have them draw pictures and dictate sentences about their character on each page.

Welcome Back!

Young children often feel a loss when their regular teacher is gone for the day. This activity gives them an opportunity to welcome their teacher back from an absence and at the same time make the teacher feel appreciated!

Invite children to write their regular teacher a cheery "welcome back" letter using the pattern on the next page. Point out the parts of a letter, such as date, greeting, body, closing, and signature. Have them personalize their greeting by writing the teacher's name on the apple's leaf.

Independent writers may compose their own letter, or you may compose a class letter for students to copy from the chalkboard. You may want to make an apple "Welcome Back!" greeting card by cutting two copies of the apple from red construction paper and placing the letter inside.

Use this pattern to write
a "Welcome Back" letter
to your teacher.

Teacher

Welcome Back!

Greeting

Date

Closing

Signature

What a Character!

Character Name: ____

Book Title: ____

By: ____

①

··

Character Traits

- My character is ___________________________.

  I know this because

  ____

  ____

- My character is ___________________________.

  I know this because

  ____

  ____

- My character is ___________________________.

  I know this because

  ____

  ____

②

What are problems your character goes through?
How does she or he solve them?

Problem	Solution

③

How is my character like me? How is she or he different from me?
Fill in the Venn diagram.

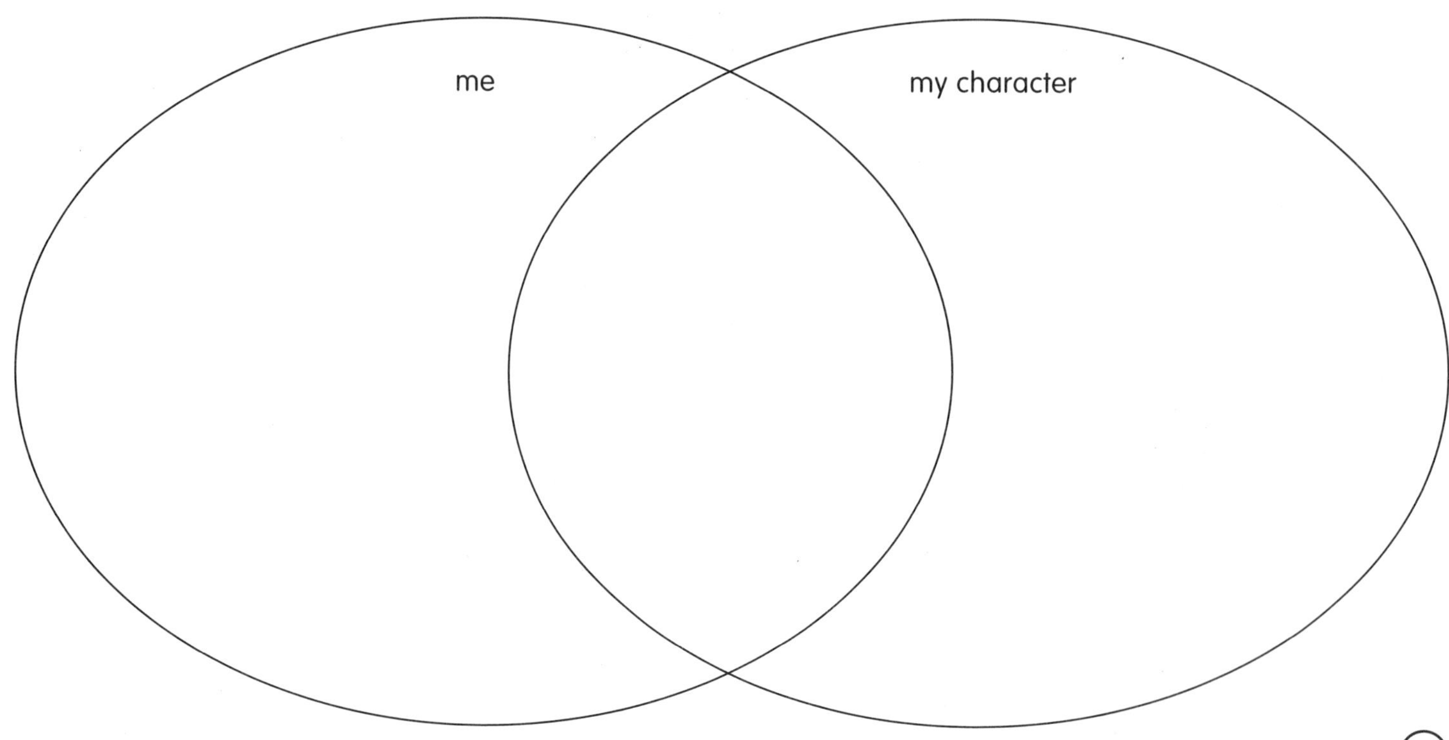

④